LITTLI
POLITICS

THE LITTLE BOOK OF POLITICS

An Hachette UK Company
www.hachette.co.uk

Summersdale Publishers Ltd
Part of Octopus Publishing Group Limited
Carmelite House
50 Victoria Embankment
LONDON
EC4Y 0DZ
UK

www.summersdale.com

Printed and bound in Malta

ISBN: 978-1-78685-516-9

The
LITTLE BOOK OF
POLITICS

Steven Gauge

Contents

SAFE IS SPELT D-U-L-L.
POLITICS HAS GOT TO
BE A FUN ACTIVITY.

ALAN CLARK

Introduction

More and more people are getting interested in politics, and politics is getting more and more interesting. As politicians find new ways of winning and using power, people everywhere are finding new ways of getting politically active. Opinions and attitudes are shifting at such a pace that the pollsters and pundits are struggling to keep up.

Politics finds its way into almost every corner of our lives. Whilst the plotting, scheming and petty point-scoring might put some off, others thrive on it. Passions rise when the issues affect people's lives. Finding out how to play your part in the political process has never mattered more.

Politics is too important to leave to the politicians, so this little book would like to warmly welcome you into the political world. It will be your handy guide as you take your first tentative steps towards becoming politically active. With a bit of the history, the things you need to know today and a few tricks of the trade, it will help you to change the world for the better and stand up for what you believe.

POLITICS IS SUPPOSED TO
BE THE SECOND-OLDEST
PROFESSION. I HAVE
COME TO REALISE THAT
IT BEARS A VERY CLOSE
RESEMBLANCE TO THE FIRST.

RONALD REAGAN

SO, WHAT IS POLITICS?

Politics is a convenient way of describing the delicate art of sorting things out when there is a wide variety of different interests at play. It's sometimes about power on an international scale, and at other times about local activists getting broken streetlamps fixed in their neighbourhood. Politics is driven by elections, but it doesn't stop there. When the votes are counted and the declarations made, there are alliances to be formed and deals to be done.

For some, politics is a dirty word, an insult or a catch-all term for the worst aspects of public life. For others, it is something to be promoted and celebrated. At the end of the day, politics is the perfectly imperfect place where public policy, power and personal ambition meet to fix things, and (whisper it quietly) many would argue that the world is a better place as a result.

THE GREEKS HAD A WORD FOR IT

The philosopher Aristotle was one of the first to have a go at talking about politics. Back in Ancient Greece, he came to the view that 'Man is by nature a political animal'. This, he decided, was mostly because, unlike other animals, we have the power of speech and can tell the difference between good and evil. Anyone who didn't want to take part in politics was, in Aristotle's view, either an outcast, a lover of war or like a bird flying alone. An Ancient Greek city or city-state was known as a *polis*, and so politics was literally the affairs of cities.

THE SCIENCE OF POLITICS

The American academic Harold Lasswell wrote a book about politics in 1936, and its very title became the go-to definition for political scientists. It was called *Politics: Who Gets What, When, How.* In other words, he argued that politics was about power and the distribution of resources.

Universities all around the world take great pleasure in seeking to explain how politics really works, whilst mostly making it utterly incomprehensible. Scholars grapple with the intricacies of political theory, and think about how politicians interact with civil servants and campaigning groups and why people vote the way they do. Acres of forest have been pulped to produce the political books and journals that help to fill academic libraries, but in the real world politics moves on quite quickly. Often, the elegant theories of the scholars are wildly out of date before the ink has dried.

In short, you don't need a politics degree to enjoy politics or engage in political debate!

HISTORY IS PAST POLITICS.
POLITICS IS PRESENT HISTORY.

E. A. FREEMAN

UK POLITICS BY NUMBERS

Before we probe too deeply into some more intimate details of how British politics works, let's have a look at the numbers. As you will see, they all add up to explain how politics finds its way into so many aspects of our lives.

1	Monarch (is supposed to be 'above politics', so tops this list)
117	Government ministers
650	Members of Parliament (533 from English constituencies, 59 from Scotland, 40 from Wales and 18 from Northern Ireland)
*c.*800	Members of the House of Lords (Peers)
129	Members of the Scottish Parliament

90	Members of the Northern Ireland Assembly
60	Members of the National Assembly for Wales
418	Local authorities
c.21,000	Local authority councillors
c.11,000	Parish, town, community and neighbourhood councils
c.80,000	Parish, town, community and neighbourhood councillors (in England)
c.46 MILLION	Registered voters
c.66 MILLION	Population of the UK

TIMING IS EVERYTHING

General elections used to happen whenever the prime minister decided to nip round to Buckingham Palace and ask the monarch to dissolve Parliament. Each election had to be within five years of the last one, but often they would happen sooner than that. If the prime minister thought things were looking good, they might call an election early. Alternatively, if things were going badly and they lost something called a 'vote of confidence' in the House of Commons, they would have to have an early election whether they wanted one or not.

The Fixed Term Parliaments Act (2011) changed all that. Elections now happen on the first Thursday in May every five years, but there can still be a snap election if two-thirds of MPs vote for one. That's what happened in 2017.

GENERAL ELECTION TIMETABLE

After the prime minister visits the monarch to ask them to dissolve Parliament, they announce the general election date to the world's media from outside 10 Downing Street. The following timetable then kicks in:

PROROGATION

All the loose ends of the last Parliament's business are tidied up in a strange ceremony. A list of the new pieces of legislation that have been agreed upon is read out, and a clerk declares that *'La Reyne le veult'* – Norman French for 'The Queen wills it'. This is not at all silly.

DAY 0: DISSOLUTION OF PARLIAMENT

The official campaign timetable starts as MPs vacate the Palace of Westminster and legal documents are issued to call the election in each of the 650 constituencies around the UK.

DAY 6: DELIVERY OF NOMINATION PAPERS

Every candidate has to find ten different registered electors in their constituency to sign their nomination papers. They then have to hand their forms in to the 'returning officer', the local council boss who has been put in charge of running the election in that area.

DAY 13: VOTER REGISTRATION DEADLINE

This is your last chance to make sure that your name is on the electoral register so that you can vote. It's easiest to do this online (www.gov.uk/register-to-vote), and it takes about 5 minutes. You don't need to register separately for every election, but you do need to register again if you've changed your address, name or nationality.

DAY 14: POSTAL VOTE APPLICATION DEADLINE

It is easy to vote by post and lots of people do. You can ask for an application on the voter registration website mentioned earlier. It makes life easier if you are too busy or insufficiently mobile to get to your polling station, or if you are going to be busy helping your favourite party on polling day in some capacity or other.

DAY 25: POLLING DAY

Polling stations are open from 7 a.m. to 10 p.m. You should receive a polling card in the post, which tells you which polling station to go to. You don't need your polling card or any other ID to vote (but you do need photo ID if you live in Northern Ireland). Candidates and their campaign teams spend the day reminding their supporters to vote.

'FIRST PAST THE POST'

There are lots of different ways of running elections, but the system favoured for electing MPs in the UK is called 'First Past the Post'. It's a bit like a horse race in that respect.

A total of 650 seats in the House of Commons are up for grabs. That is one seat for each parliamentary constituency. A constituency is an area made up of 75,000 or so voters. It is meant to represent a natural community, and there are independent boundary commissions to tweak the boundaries every now and again.

All the different candidates' names and their parties go onto the ballot papers and the voter simply puts one cross next to their favourite candidate. Whoever gets the most votes becomes the MP. Whichever party then has the most MPs normally forms the government.

Not everyone likes the system, and smaller parties in particular can be disadvantaged by it. If, for example, one party came second or third in every constituency, it might have lots of votes, but it would still have no **MPs**. Fans of the system argue that it is simple, easily understood and leads to strong governments.

PEOPLE WHO ARE NOT ALLOWED TO STAND FOR PARLIAMENT:

☞ Civil servants

☞ Members of police forces

☞ Members of the armed forces

☞ Judges

☞ Members of the legislature of any country or territory outside the Commonwealth

☞ Peers who are entitled to sit and vote in the House of Lords (known as the 'Lords temporal')

☞ Bishops of the Church of England who are entitled to sit and vote in the House of Lords (known as the 'Lords spiritual')

☞ Anyone who is in prison serving a sentence of a year or more

☞ Anyone who has broken election rules in the previous five years

PARLIAMENTARY CANDIDATES MUST BE:

☞ Over 18 years old

☞ British citizens or citizens of a Commonwealth country or the Republic of Ireland

☞ Able to put up a £500 deposit (which they will lose if they get less than 5 per cent of the votes cast)

And each candidate can only stand in one constituency at a time!

A POSTHUMOUS POLITICAL SWANSONG

Ronnie Carroll twice represented the United Kingdom in the Eurovision Song Contest in the 1960s, finishing fourth on both occasions. Later in life, he stood for Parliament with the declared ambition of becoming the first candidate to secure no votes, or, in Eurovision parlance, *nul points*. In April 2015 he died just a few days after handing in his nomination papers to stand in the general election as a candidate for Hampstead and Kilburn. The election would have been postponed if he had been standing for a registered party, but as he was an independent the election went ahead with Ronnie's name still on the ballot papers. The late Ronnie Carroll secured a grand total of 113 votes – 26 votes more than seventh-placed candidate Robin Ellison, who had the advantage, you would have thought, of being alive on polling day.

THE
MOTHER OF
PARLIAMENTS

DEMOCRACY IS THE WORST
FORM OF GOVERNMENT
EXCEPT FOR ALL THOSE
OTHERS THAT HAVE BEEN
TRIED FROM TIME TO TIME.

WINSTON CHURCHILL

A MODEL PARLIAMENT

The streets of Westminster are always lined with tourists taking selfies alongside the Houses of Parliament, especially the part that is officially named the Elizabeth Tower, but is known to everyone by the nickname of Big Ben. What goes on inside the world-famous building shapes our laws and changes our lives. The way it does so is known by academics as the 'Westminster model', which has been copied all around the world.

It is called the Houses (plural) of Parliament because there are two 'houses' within the building. The House of Commons is where all the elected MPs sit on green benches. The House of Lords is where all appointed and hereditary peers sit on red benches. For any law to change, both houses have to agree. If you want to sound terribly clever, you can also call this a 'bicameral system'.

After a general election, both houses come together, with MPs squeezing into one end of the Lords chamber to hear the 'Gracious Speech', where the monarch reads out what the winning party plans to do in the coming Parliament. From there, the process of making new laws and governing the country begins.

LAYING DOWN THE LAW

For most of us, a bill is one of those things that comes in a brown envelope or email and hurts our bank balance. For parliamentarians, a bill is a proposed set of new laws that gets debated and amended and debated again. Once the bill has been shaped into a set of words that both Houses of Parliament can agree on, the monarch gives approval in what is grandly referred to as 'royal assent'. It then becomes an Act of Parliament. It is printed onto vellum parchment made from calfskin, and is stored in the Victoria Tower at one end of the Palace of Westminster (another name for the Houses of Parliament). Maybe if all our household bills were printed on vellum, we might not forget to pay them.

HOW BILLS BECOME ACTS

FIRST READING

The title of the bill is read out in the Commons
and the date of the second reading is
decided. This just takes a few seconds.

SECOND READING

The bill is debated in the Commons. MPs vote to
decide whether the bill should move on to...

COMMITTEE STAGE

A cross-party committee of MPs goes through the bill
line by line, changing the bits it doesn't like.

REPORT STAGE

Back to the Commons for more debate
and more changes.

THIRD READING

A final short debate before sending it off to the
House of Lords to start the same process all over
again (conversely, some bills start their life in the
Lords and come to the Commons afterwards).

CONSIDERATION OF AMENDMENTS

Both houses have to agree each other's changes, known
as 'ping-pong' because politicians bat the bill back and
forth. If both houses can't agree, the Commons can use
the rules laid down in the Parliament Acts of 1911 and
1949 to get their own way in any event.

ROYAL ASSENT

The monarch formally agrees the bill, which becomes
an Act of Parliament and therefore the law.

THE GREASY POLE

The Houses of Parliament also provide a recruiting ground for the government, as every minister must also be either an MP or a peer. The prime minister of the day appoints over a hundred government ministers, including just over 20 Cabinet members (the exact number can vary). This is the top tier of British politics. The Cabinet usually meets weekly around an awkwardly thin boardroom-style table, where they decide on the government's policies. Beneath the Cabinet is a layer of junior ministers, each with their own bit of public policy to look after. Beneath the junior ministers is a group of MPs appointed as parliamentary private secretaries (PPSs), an unpaid role seen as the first rung on the ministerial career ladder.

The party with the most MPs normally forms the government, although sometimes they might need to obtain the support of one or two smaller parties. The leader of the second-largest party becomes Leader of the opposition and appoints a Shadow Cabinet. The job of an opposition MP is to keep tabs on the government minister they have been appointed to shadow, and to be their party's spokesperson on their allotted subject.

Government ministers and ministries chop and change their titles and responsibilities quite regularly but, alongside the prime minister, three top jobs stay pretty much the same: Chancellor of the Exchequer, Foreign Secretary and Home Secretary. Collectively, they are known as the 'Great Offices of State'. They come with pretty swanky offices too.

Prime Minister: gets to live at 10 Downing Street, appoint and chair the Cabinet, and meet up with the monarch once a week for a little chat. Oh yes, and run the country.

Chancellor of the Exchequer: twice a year, they get their photo in all the papers holding up a red briefcase containing the national budget (their statement to Parliament about the nation's finances and any tax changes). Runs the Treasury and holds the purse strings. Lives next door to the PM at 11 Downing Street.

Foreign Secretary: as head of the Foreign and Commonwealth Office, gets to travel the world. Has oversight of the spooks at GCHQ and MI6 and at the weekends gets to entertain foreign dignitaries at the country estate of Chevening in Kent.

Home Secretary: responsible for internal affairs, in particular immigration, citizenship, policing and national security. Used to run prisons too, but that now falls under the Ministry of Justice. The national security service MI5 reports to the Home Secretary.

All Cabinet and Shadow Cabinet members sit on the front benches of the House of Commons chamber during debates. Other MPs sit on the rows behind them and are therefore known as 'backbenchers'.

THE HOUSE OF COMMONS: A DIAGRAM

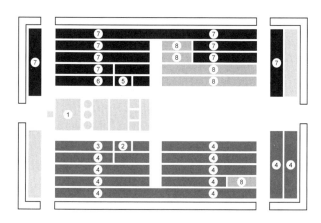

❶ Speaker – one of the MPs, chosen to chair the debates

❷ Prime minister

❸ Government ministers

❹ Government back benches

❺ Leader of the Opposition

❻ Shadow ministers

❼ Opposition back benches

❽ Other parties

QUESTIONS, QUESTIONS, QUESTIONS

Politicians often talk about 'holding the government to account'. It's a bit of jargon that basically means asking difficult questions to keep the government in check. Prime Minister's Questions (PMQs) is one of the big set-piece events of the political week. Every Wednesday at noon, the PM answers questions from MPs in a packed Commons chamber for half an hour (although the current Speaker seems to add quite a bit of 'injury time'). Opposition MPs will try to catch the PM out, whilst loyal government backbenchers will try to win favour by giving their leader an easy question and a chance to shine. It's all great theatre, and it's where political careers are made or broken.

Ministers of government departments also have to face their own sets of questions at different times. There are oral questions across the chamber and written questions where the answers are published in public documents. There are committees where MPs ask questions of ministers, civil servants and invited witnesses. When they are not asking questions in the Commons, MPs will write letters to ministers, on behalf of their constituents, asking yet more questions.

THE DARK ARTS...

The job of keeping MPs in order falls to a group of characters with a shady reputation. They are known 'affectionately' as 'party whips'. These are MPs and lords who are appointed to make sure that all their party members turn out and vote the right way at the right time on the big issues. They act as their party leader's eyes and ears in the chamber. If the backbenchers are unhappy with their leader, the party whips are usually the first to know.

Whips get their name from an eighteenth-century hunting term. The 'whipper-in' was the hunt assistant whose job was to crack a whip in order to round up any hounds straying from the pack. Parliamentary whips have to use more gentle powers of persuasion to drag their straying party members back into line nowadays. They might dangle the prospect of ministerial promotion or threaten to reveal some little-known indiscretion to get their way. Voters tend not to like parties that appear divided, so it is down to the whips to ensure that any disagreements are aired in private.

THE HOUSE OF LORDS

The House of Lords is made up of roughly 800 members, most of whom are 'life peers'. That means they have been appointed to the job for life, but don't get to pass the title on to their children. Unlike MPs, they don't have to stand for election. Former ministers and MPs are often given a life peerage, as are the so-called 'great and good' from a variety of walks of life. An independent House of Lords Appointments Commission recommends and vets the nominees. The monarch officially appoints the peers on the advice of the prime minister of the day.

There are also 'hereditary peers'. These are members of the aristocracy who inherited their titles going back many generations. They used to all have the right to a seat in the House of Lords until reforms in 1999 restricted them to 92 seats. If one of them dies, they have an election amongst themselves to choose a replacement.

Twenty-six Church of England bishops and archbishops also have seats in the House of Lords.

CROSS-BENCHERS

The peers see their role as that of a revising chamber. They take great pride in their ability to look at the fine detail of pieces of legislation, spot potential problems and make corrections in the form of carefully crafted amendments. They also seem to be much happier than MPs, probably because they don't have to face the public in an election every few years.

The House of Lords has a slightly different layout to the House of Commons, and a very different atmosphere. The debates are a lot less heated and peers tend to listen to one another politely and quietly. Whilst most peers are nominated by the political parties they represent, a large number are independent. These independent peers are referred to as 'cross-benchers', not because they are prone to bad moods, but because they sit on the benches that stretch across the chamber between the government and opposition ranks.

WHAT ARE MEMBERS OF PARLIAMENT (MPS) FOR?

BEING AN MP IS THE SORT OF JOB ALL WORKING-CLASS PARENTS WANT FOR THEIR CHILDREN — CLEAN, INDOORS AND NO HEAVY LIFTING.

DIANE ABBOTT

A WEEK IN THE LIFE OF AN MP

Being an MP is not like any ordinary job. There is no job description and no employment contract. There is no probation period, no appraisal system and no key performance indicators. Instead, there's just lots of politics. A typical week could include any of the following:

- ☞ Holding 'surgeries' in their constituency, which are sessions where residents come and raise their concerns.

- ☞ Writing emails and letters on behalf of constituents.

- ☞ Travelling to and from London, the distance depending on where their constituency is.

- ☞ Attending committees and scrutinising legislation.

- ☞ Attending parliamentary party meetings.

- ☞ Speaking in debates.

- ☞ Voting (MPs vote by physically walking into either the 'yes' or 'no' lobby adjacent to the chamber

– an antiquated tradition but it also gives them a chance to catch up with one another, and perhaps even lobby ministers on the local issues of their own constituencies).

- ☞ Chairing an All-Party Parliamentary Group on a particular issue.

- ☞ Meeting campaigning groups and organisations.

- ☞ Taking constituents on tours of Parliament.

- ☞ Asking questions of ministers in the chamber.

- ☞ Being interviewed by the media.

- ☞ Attending charity events and photo opportunities.

- ☞ Researching around policy issues and preparing for debates.

- ☞ Campaigning in the constituency with local party activists.

- ☞ Visiting local community groups.

- ☞ Attending party fundraising events.

- ☞ Managing a small team of paid staff and volunteers.

MONEY FOR OLD ROPE?

Members of Parliament are paid around £70,000 per year, but what do we get for our money? Each MP is their own boss, so they largely get to decide what they do and how they do it. They do come under lots of pressure from their own party, their constituents and the media to do various things in certain ways, but ultimately it's up to them how they use their time. Broadly speaking, the job of being an MP can be split into three distinct roles:

- ☞ **Parliamentarian:** helping to generate new laws and amend old ones, whether supporting the government or challenging from the opposition benches.

- ☞ **Community champion:** speaking up for the people who elected them and the constituency they represent, and helping individuals to sort out their everyday problems.

- ☞ **Party representative:** developing and promoting political ideas and policies, contesting elections and helping their party to gain or hold on to power.

PARLIAMENTARIAN

Being an effective parliamentarian is about having razor-sharp debating skills, an understanding of the rules of the game and the ability to spot the perfect political moment to challenge a minister. It is about using parliamentary procedures and building alliances to change the law of the land. It takes patience and persistence, and those who get it right leave a lasting legacy of their time on the political stage.

The Spectator magazine runs an annual awards evening to celebrate our politicians. One of the most hotly contested awards is for 'Parliamentarian of the Year'. In 2017 it went to Ruth Davidson, the leader of the Conservatives in Scotland, whose performance in the Scottish Parliament has been credited with reviving Tory fortunes north of the border. Labour's Hilary Benn won in 2016 for a moving speech against his own party leader in the debate on whether Britain should intervene in Syria.

PRIVATE MEMBERS' BILLS

Members of Parliament have the opportunity to enter what is probably the most exclusive lottery in the country, but there is no cash prize for the winner. Instead, a few lucky MPs will get the chance, and the parliamentary time, to get their own personal hobby horse debated in the chamber and maybe change the law as a result.

Once every Parliament session, MPs enter their names into a draw. The first seven names drawn out of the hat are granted a whole day's debate on a new bill of their choosing. If they are lucky in the ballot and have chosen a worthy issue, they may get their bill all the way through both Houses of Parliament and into law.

Significant changes that have happened as a result of private members' bills have included the abolition of the death penalty in 1965 and the legalisation of abortion in 1967. In the 20 years between 1997 and 2017, 92 of the 147 bills that were successful in the ballot went on to gain royal assent.

SCRUTINY

Parliamentarians will often use the word 'scrutiny' to describe what they get up to, and it is an important skill at every level of politics.

Scrutiny is the art of asking the right questions and getting the answers you need. Every government and council needs plenty of scrutiny to keep it on its toes. MPs get to hone their scrutiny skills by putting formal questions to ministers, including the prime minister, either in writing or in set-piece moments of political theatre in the chamber. Ministers, however, can get quite good at not giving away too much information.

DENNIS SKINNER:

HOW MANY CIVIL SERVANTS ARE A) MEN AND B) WOMEN?

TIM RENTON:

ALL OF THEM.

COMMUNITY CHAMPION

Whilst most people will tell opinion pollsters that they don't really like MPs as a species, they quite often like their own local MP. Often that's because their MP has worked out how to be a good constituency MP and, therefore, a community champion. A local MP has the perfect opportunity to become a spokesperson for their area, to be someone who leads the fight for local services and improvements on their patch.

Most MPs run so-called 'surgeries' in their constituencies. They won't take out your appendix or fix your ingrowing toenail, but they might write a sternly worded letter on your behalf, making full use of their very grand parliamentary headed paper. The House of Commons logo of a crowned portcullis does seem to have a magical effect on some local council and government department bureaucrats, so it really can help to get people's problems resolved a little more promptly.

PARTY REPRESENTATIVE

Politics is a two-way process. MPs must be the voice of the people, amplifying their views and sharing their concerns, but they must also have the vision to inspire those same people. For most politicians, the vision thing comes from within their party, because a truly independent MP is a real rarity in Britain. Most politicians are party players, and promoting their party on the doorstep is an important part of their job.

The party machine will help MPs to get elected, but it will expect something in return. Its MPs will be expected to organise things behind the scenes, help shape party policies, raise money to fund party campaigns and loyally support the party at all times, even when they think the party has got something wrong.

Truly successful MPs, then, are the ones who can combine the roles of parliamentarian and community champion with the demands of party politics.

EXPENSES SCANDAL

In 2009, an expenses scandal erupted in British politics that was so high profile that even people with absolutely no interest in politics knew about it. MPs of all parties were shown to have fiddled the system set up to reimburse them for the day-to-day costs of being an elected representative. One MP attempted to claim for a floating duck house in his garden, another for the cost of cleaning his moat. Some MPs were found to have used their allowances – meant to fund the cost of having somewhere to stay near Westminster – to make huge amounts of money on the property market.

The worst offenders in the expenses scandal were seriously punished at the ballot box in the election that followed in 2010. A handful of MPs were even imprisoned for false accounting and fraud, and the scandal brought an ignominious end to a number of political careers. The Independent Parliamentary Standards Authority now regulates and publishes all MP expenses.

THE PHILOSOPHERS HAVE ONLY INTERPRETED THE WORLD, IN VARIOUS WAYS; THE POINT IS TO CHANGE IT.

KARL MARX

DOES VOTING CHANGE ANYTHING?

Sadly, many people are reluctant voters, because they don't trust politicians to deliver on their promises. Many argue that, whichever political party wins, nothing really changes as 'they are all just the same'. Voter turnout slumped to just 59.4 per cent in 2001. Although it has risen a bit since then, it was still only 68.7 per cent in the 2017 general election. So, does voting matter and does it make a difference to people's lives?

REASONS TO BE CHEERFUL?

There are many aspects of our society that we all treasure today which have come about because of politics. Laws governing how people are treated at work, who they can marry, where they live and what they can buy have all been influenced by politicians. And each politician got their job because of the crosses that voters placed on ballot papers in polling stations all around the country. Here are just a few examples of ways the world has changed and how politicians made them happen. You might like some changes and not others, but no one can deny that politics has made a huge difference to all of our lives.

THE NHS

The National Health Service (NHS) was founded on 5 July 1948, but the impetus for its creation stemmed from the Labour Party's landslide election victory of 1945. There had been talk of healthcare reform for decades before then, but nothing had actually happened.

Champion of 'the Left' and a political big-hitter, Aneurin (Nye) Bevan had been appointed as Minister of Health. With a strong electoral mandate, he was able to take on vested interests such as the British Medical Association, who wanted to have a system funded by insurance. A letter in the BMA journal went so far as to describe Bevan as a 'complete and uncontrolled dictator'. Bevan later said his opponents had helped to cement the popularity of his creation, because a fear that insurance charges might otherwise be introduced led to a flood of patients using the fledgling NHS.

To gain the crucial support of doctors and nurses, Bevan allowed GPs to retain the freedom to run their own practices. Hospital consultants were given more money, and nurses' pay was also increased to attract recruits. Bevan admitted later, 'I stuffed their mouths with gold.'

The NHS was the first health system in any Western society to offer free medical care to the entire population, funded through general taxation. Its first year's budget was £437 million – around £15 billion at today's prices. Today, £147.5 billion is spent on health across the UK – roughly ten times what was spent in 1948/49.

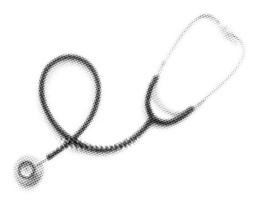

THE RIGHT TO BUY

When Margaret Thatcher walked into 10 Downing Street as Conservative prime minister in 1979, she had persuaded large numbers of people to change the way they voted. One of the key manifesto pledges that had helped to win over crucial working-class votes had been a promise to give council tenants the right to buy their home at a large discount. In England alone, 970,000 homes were sold by the time she had to resign as leader of the party in 1990.

'Right to buy' has remained hugely controversial. Opponents have been angered by the reduction in the stock of social housing, as local authorities were prevented from using the receipts to create more homes. Margaret Thatcher's fans, on the other hand, point out that she increased home ownership. The number of owner-occupiers went from 10.2 million in the 1981 census to 14.9 million in 2011.

For many young people today, getting onto the housing ladder seems almost impossible. Planning policy and local government funding restrictions have meant that new social housing to rent is in short supply. Rising homelessness and lengthening waiting lists have led to desperate measures. A BBC report in 2017 found that some councils have spent millions buying back homes that they had previously sold under the right-to-buy legislation. Housing seems set to be a major political issue for many years to come.

EGGS

Politics can find its way into every aspect of our lives and there are no egg-ceptions to that rule (sorry). In the 1980s, there was a cosy working relationship between the farming industry and their regulators. The egg-producers had a bit of a problem with a nasty bug called salmonella, which was finding its way into eggs. The Ministry of Agriculture, Fisheries and Food felt that as long as everyone cooked their eggs properly, with no runny yolks, there was no need for any further regulation.

Edwina Currie, a junior health minister at the time, disagreed. She went on TV and declared that most eggs had salmonella in them, causing outrage from the farming industry. The ensuing uproar cost Edwina Currie her political career, but the scandal led to a dramatic shift in the standards within the industry. A new kite-marking system was introduced, and in 2017 the egg industry in the UK was finally declared completely salmonella-free. So, thanks to one politician sacrificing her career, you can now have a soft-boiled egg without risking your health.

A DOG'S BREAKFAST

Parliamentarians don't always get it right when drafting legislation, especially when it is done in a hurry. The Dangerous Dogs Act (1991) is a classic example.

In the early nineties, there were harrowing tales of dog attacks on young children. Pit bull terriers and Rottweilers were often blamed. The result of public and media pressure was the Dangerous Dogs Act. It became illegal to own certain types of dogs, and sanctions were introduced on the owners of any dogs that were dangerously out of control.

However, the Act's definitions were unclear. It banned 'the type of dog known as the pit bull'. Teams of experts have battled it out in court to determine if a dog's legs were too short or its ears pointy enough to be classified as dangerous. In one case, a boxer-collie cross was sentenced to death for barking at a postman. The Act was amended in 1997, but confusion and criticism continue. Tragic cases still arise of children being attacked and sometimes killed by domestic pets.

ALL POLITICS IS LOCAL.

THOMAS (TIP) O'NEILL

KEEPING
IT LOCAL

Politics isn't just about what goes on in Westminster. In town halls and council chambers all around the country, the political battles are just as passionate and, for many people, all the more important. Here is a guide to the different layers of government and their varied powers and responsibilities.

PARISH AND TOWN COUNCILS

There are over 9,000 parish or town councils in England. They are the first tier of local government and have limited powers, but they can still have a real impact locally. They are often less 'party political', with independent candidates regularly elected and fewer votes along party lines. They normally have a very small budget, perhaps employing only one person as a town or parish clerk, but they do fund local improvements, such as a park bench or grit bins, and they often run community events. More often than not, they get very involved in local planning applications.

DISTRICT COUNCILS

The next tier of local government is the district council. Here, elected local councillors can get their teeth into a wider range of public services – like rubbish collection, recycling, planning decisions and housing – and have a grander stage for their political ambitions. Each district is divided up into electoral wards of around 7,000 people, with each ward electing either two or three councillors. Some councils elect all their councillors in one go every four years. Others elect their councillors a third at a time, with just one councillor out of three in every ward coming up for election in any particular year, for three years out of the four available. Each councillor serves for four years before having to stand for re-election. In those districts that hold elections in thirds, local political parties are in almost permanent political campaigning mode.

COUNTY COUNCILS

County councils have more power, more money and more to do. They look after education, social services, libraries and transport. County councillors are elected to cover larger areas known as divisions, which are made up of a number of district council wards. A local county councillor will often be quite a big cheese within their local party hierarchy. They might be a district and/or a parish councillor as well. County councils have their elections every four years, normally when the districts that elect by 'thirds' in their area are having a year off.

UNITARY AUTHORITIES

As if it wasn't confusing enough, there are some areas where they have a different structure altogether, having only one layer of local government that does everything that districts and counties elsewhere do separately. Around the rest of the country there are areas where district councils have claimed the powers of the county and started running things for themselves. In other places, county councils have gobbled up all their local districts and created one great big organisation that does everything.

MAYORS

Mayors used to be exclusively elected by local councillors from among their own number, and many still are. They normally serve for one year at a time, get to wear robes and chains and funny hats, and are mainly responsible for chairing council meetings and opening local fetes and garden parties. This sort of mayor is known as a civic mayor, but now there is a new kid on the block.

Local government reforms have created a role known as a directly elected mayor. They are directly elected by the public across a wide area, such as an entire borough, town, city or region. Quite often they are the sole political decision-maker for their area and they get to appoint a cabinet of advisers, dishing out responsibilities to them as they see fit. They are elected for longer – four years at a time – and, with a large personal mandate, tend to extend their political tentacles far and wide. London has a directly elected mayor who looks after transport and policing and, by virtue of having been elected by over a million people, has enough political clout to pronounce on pretty much anything.

DEVOLVED POWERS

Scotland, Wales and Northern Ireland all have their own devolved political institutions and separate powers. Scotland has a Parliament, whilst Wales and Northern Ireland each have an Assembly. Each has its own different electoral system and a variety of new ways to get elected.

Scotland has a mixed system, with 73 Members of the Scottish Parliament (MSPs) elected to represent constituencies, plus 56 MSPs elected across eight larger electoral regions.

The Welsh Assembly also has a mixed system, with 40 Assembly Members (AMs) elected within constituencies and another 20 elected across five regions.

Northern Ireland elects 90 Members of the Legislative Assembly (MLAs) across 18 constituencies by something called a single transferable vote system. Voters get to rank the candidates in their order of preference. This tends to give the political parties a share of the seats that is more proportional to their share of the overall vote.

The Northern Ireland Assembly also has a set of rules to ensure it includes both sides of the religious divide, so negotiations to form coalition governments can take longer as a result.

IT'S MY PARTY

ONE OF THE MYTHS OF THE BRITISH PARLIAMENT IS THAT THERE ARE THREE PARTIES THERE. I CAN ASSURE YOU FROM BITTER PERSONAL EXPERIENCE THERE ARE 629.

HORACE MAYBRAY KING, FORMER SPEAKER OF THE HOUSE OF COMMONS

Politicians do like a party. In spite of what you might read in the press, political parties are not primarily an excuse to drink excessively and behave inappropriately, although clearly that does happen from time to time. Political parties are mostly about meetings, meetings and more meetings.

As the machines that drive politics, the parties bring together people who share a set of values, more or less, and enable them to achieve more together than they ever could on their own.

Political parties come and go, and some have more staying power than others. Here is a quick beginner's guide to the current crop and their defining features.

CONSERVATIVE PARTY

☞ Founded in the 1830s by Sir Robert Peel, the Conservatives are the oldest political party in Europe.

☞ The Conservative Party was reported to have about 149,800 paid-up members as of December 2013, but the party doesn't actually keep a centrally run membership list.

☞ Known also as 'the Tories', a shorter name preferred by newspaper headline writers. The term is probably derived from the Irish word *tóraí*, meaning 'outlaw' or 'robber', and was first applied in the seventeenth century to politicians who opposed a Catholic monarchy.

IN FAVOUR OF: the free market, low inflation, lower taxes and less public spending.

AGAINST: state interference, red tape and overly powerful trade unions.

TOP 3

LONGEST-SERVING CONSERVATIVE PRIME MINISTERS*

* OF THE TWENTIETH CENTURY

Margaret Thatcher

☞ Britain's first female prime minister.

☞ Prime minister for 11 years and 209 days between 1979 and 1990 (the longest-serving British prime minister of the twentieth century).

☞ Won three general elections: 1979, 1983 and 1987.

☞ Oversaw a fundamental shift in economic policy from Keynesianism (using public spending to create jobs) towards Monetarism (reducing inflation by controlling how much money is in the economy).

☞ Took on the trade unions, notably the National Union of Mineworkers, who went on strike in 1984–85.

☞ Sent a military task force into the South Atlantic to retake the Falkland Islands from Argentina in 1982.

I DON'T MIND HOW MUCH MY MINISTERS TALK AS LONG AS THEY DO WHAT I SAY.

MARGARET THATCHER

Winston Churchill

☞ Became prime minister in May 1940 to lead Britain through the Second World War.

☞ Lost office in 1945 but remained as Conservative Party leader.

☞ Elected as prime minister again in 1951 and served until his retirement in 1955.

☞ Prime minister for a total of 8 years and 239 days.

☞ Coined the phrase 'Iron Curtain' to describe the influence of the Soviet Union on countries across Eastern Europe.

☞ Awarded the Nobel Prize for Literature in 1953 for his biographical and historical writings, including his six-volume account of the Second World War.

☞ His passing was marked by a state funeral in 1965 and he is commemorated with a statue in Parliament Square.

☞ Topped the BBC poll of the 100 Greatest Britons in 2002.

HISTORY WILL BE KIND TO ME, FOR I INTEND TO WRITE IT!

WINSTON CHURCHILL

Stanley Baldwin

☞ Prime minister on three separate occasions: 1923–24; 1924–29; 1935–37.

☞ Resident at 10 Downing Street for a total of 7 years and 82 days.

☞ Proclaimed a state of emergency during the General Strike of 1926.

☞ His electoral victory in 1935 was the last time that any political party has ever achieved more than 50 per cent of the vote.

☞ Introduced the Public Order Act (1936) following marches by the British Union of Fascists and their opponents.

YOU WILL FIND IN POLITICS
THAT YOU ARE MUCH EXPOSED
TO THE ATTRIBUTION OF FALSE
MOTIVE. NEVER COMPLAIN
AND NEVER EXPLAIN.

STANLEY BALDWIN

LABOUR PARTY

- ☞ Formed in 1900 by the Trades Union Congress as the Labour Representation Committee to support working-class MPs.

- ☞ Their first leader was Keir Hardie, a Scottish miner and trade unionist who had been elected as an independent MP for West Ham.

- ☞ Many Labour members would describe themselves as socialists, in favour of the common ownership of the means of production and exchange – i.e. lots of nationalised industries. Others would call themselves social democrats, with a greater emphasis on issues of social justice.

- ☞ As of June 2017, Labour had 552,000 members, making it Western Europe's largest political party.

IN FAVOUR OF: redistribution of income and wealth, public sector spending generally (particularly on the NHS) and equality.

AGAINST: poverty, unemployment and the private sector profiting from public services.

TOP 3
LONGEST-SERVING LABOUR PRIME MINISTERS

Tony Blair

- ☞ Prime minister for 10 years and 56 days between 1997 and 2007.

- ☞ Created 'New Labour' to attract middle-class voters and end Labour's 18 years in opposition.

- ☞ Devolved power to a Scottish Parliament and a Welsh Assembly.

- ☞ Steered Northern Ireland through the final stages of the Good Friday Peace Agreement in 1998.

- ☞ Introduced the Freedom of Information Act (1997) and the National Minimum Wage Act (1998).

- ☞ Reputation damaged by his decision to take the country to war against Iraq in pursuit of weapons of mass destruction that were never found.

ASK ME MY THREE MAIN PRIORITIES FOR GOVERNMENT, AND I TELL YOU: EDUCATION, EDUCATION AND EDUCATION.

TONY BLAIR

Harold Wilson

☞ Served two separate terms as prime minister: 1964–70 and 1974–76.

☞ Held the highest office for a total of 7 years and 279 days.

☞ Won four of the five general elections he fought as Labour Party leader.

☞ Famous for his trademark pipe, seeking to boost the economy with the 'white heat' of modern technology and being forced to devalue the pound in 1967.

☞ Ended capital punishment, decriminalised homosexuality and introduced the Race Relations Act (1965) and the Equal Pay Act (1970).

☞ Pushed through the creation of the Open University in 1969, in spite of it not actually appearing in the Labour election manifesto.

☞ Steered Britain to a 'yes' vote to remain in the European Common Market in a 1975 referendum (the first referendum ever to be held in the United Kingdom).

☞ His governments built homes at a rate of 400,000 a year.

A WEEK IS A LONG TIME IN POLITICS.

HAROLD WILSON

Ramsay MacDonald

☞ Opposed Britain's participation in the First World War.

☞ Became Labour's first prime minister in 1924 as head of a minority government. That term of office, supported by the Liberals, lasted for just 287 days.

☞ His second term lasted longer, from 1929 to 1935.

☞ In 1931, during the Great Depression, he headed a 'National Government' dominated by the Conservative Party and supported by only a few Labour MPs.

☞ Served as prime minister for a total of 6 years and 289 days.

☞ Introduced legislation to improve housing and social insurance.

☞ Continually scarred by attacks from press barons and internal party splits.

WARS ARE POPULAR. CONTRACTORS MAKE PROFITS; THE ARISTOCRACY GLEAN HONOUR.

RAMSAY MacDONALD

OTHER PARTIES

It is generally accepted that the UK has a two-party system. We have had either a Labour or a Conservative prime minister since 1922. Nevertheless, other political parties are available, and they are always nipping at the heels of the big two.

Every now and again, one of the smaller parties gets a taste of power. They sometimes have a role as a junior partner in a coalition or other pact if the larger parties have both failed to get an overall majority of the seats in Parliament. Sometimes their ideas become so popular that they end up being implemented anyway, like the UKIP policy to leave the EU. As for the future of these parties and their policies, who knows? In politics, anything is possible.

SCOTTISH NATIONAL PARTY

☞ Formed in 1934 with the merger of the National Party of Scotland and the Scottish Party.

☞ First Westminster MP was Robert McIntyre, elected in 1945.

☞ Had a political breakthrough in 2007, becoming the largest single party in the Scottish Parliament. Their leader, Alex Salmond, became First Minister of Scotland.

☞ Won an overall majority in the Scottish Parliament in 2011.

☞ Held but narrowly lost a referendum on Scottish independence in September 2014 (55.3 per cent voted to remain in the United Kingdom against the 44.7 per cent who voted for independence).

☞ Won 56 of Scotland's 59 Westminster constituencies in 2015.

☞ Membership reported to be approximately 118,000 (August 2017).

LIBERAL DEMOCRATS

☞ Formed in 1988 with the merger of the Liberal Party and the Social Democratic Party (SDP).

☞ The Liberal Party had a much longer history than the SDP, but their last prime minister, David Lloyd George, left office as long ago as 1922.

☞ Opposition to the Iraq War under the leadership of Charles Kennedy saw them win 62 Westminster seats in 2005.

☞ Formed a coalition government with the Conservatives in 2010 after winning 57 seats – their leader, Nick Clegg, was appointed deputy prime minister.

☞ Entering a coalition with the Conservatives cost them dearly at the next election in 2015, after which they ended up with just eight MPs.

☞ Opposed Britain leaving the European Union.

☞ Membership is around 103,000 (September 2017).

THE POLITICAL PARTIES OF NORTHERN IRELAND

Politics in Northern Ireland runs along religious and sectarian divides, the two main parties being the Democratic Unionist Party (DUP), who want to remain a part of the UK, and Sinn Féin, who continue to seek a united Ireland. As a result, Northern Ireland has tended to get overlooked on the mainland by political pundits and academics alike. However, the hung Parliament that followed the 2017 general election brought Northern Irish politics back into sharp focus, when the ten **DUP MPs** entered a so-called 'confidence and supply' arrangement with the minority Conservative government (see next page).

DEMOCRATIC UNIONIST PARTY

☞ Formed in 1971 in the midst of 'the Troubles', the name given to the conflict between republicans seeking a united Ireland and unionists wanting to remain part of the UK.

☞ 'Ulster Says No!' was the cry of its founder and leader Dr Ian Paisley, who resisted any attempt at reconciliation with Catholics in Northern Ireland and the Irish Republic.

☞ In 2007, after years of political stalemate in the Northern Ireland Assembly (established following the Good Friday Peace Agreement of 1998), Paisley finally formed a devolved government in Northern Ireland with the republican Sinn Féin party.

☞ The 'confidence and supply' agreement with the minority Conservative government in Westminster in 2017 meant that the DUP promised to support the prime minister in any 'votes of confidence' and to support the budgets put forward by the Conservatives. In return, the government promised to invest an extra £1 billion in hospitals, schools and roads in Northern Ireland.

SINN FEIN

☞ Formed in 1905, initially favouring passive resistance to English rule.

☞ Operates as a single organisation across the Republic of Ireland and Northern Ireland.

☞ Historically, had close links to the Irish Republican Army (IRA), but emerged as a political force in the early 1980s.

☞ Led by Gerry Adams between 1983 and 2018.

☞ Sinn Féin's Martin McGuinness served as Deputy First Minister of Northern Ireland alongside the DUP from 2007 to 2017.

☞ Won seven seats in the UK Parliament in the 2017 general election, but does not take up its seats at Westminster (as that would involve pledging allegiance to the British monarch).

OTHER POLITICAL PARTIES IN NORTHERN IRELAND

Other political parties operate in Northern Ireland and have seats in its Assembly, although in 2017 none were successful in winning seats in the Westminster Parliament. On the Protestant side, there is the Ulster Unionist Party (UUP); on the Catholic side, there is the Social Democrat and Labour Party (SDLP). Seeking to bridge the sectarian divide is the Alliance Party. The Green Party, Traditional Unionist Voice and People Before Profit have also secured seats in the Northern Ireland Assembly.

PLAID CYMRU – PARTY OF WALES

☞ Formed in 1925 with the principal aims of promotion of the Welsh language and political independence for Wales.

☞ Won its first seat at Westminster in a by-election in 1966.

☞ Won four parliamentary seats at Westminster in 1992 and has maintained a similar level of representation ever since.

☞ Joined a coalition in the Welsh Assembly in 2007 with Labour.

☞ Instigated a referendum, which in 2011 secured additional legislative powers for the Welsh Assembly.

☞ Membership of about 8,300 (2017).

GREEN PARTY

☞ Inspired by a *Playboy* magazine article about overpopulation that was read by a group of friends in the Napton Bridge Inn in Warwickshire.

☞ Formed as the PEOPLE Party in 1972, renamed as the Ecology Party in 1975 and became the Green Party in 1985.

☞ It chose not to have a leader for many years, opting instead to have two 'principal speakers'.

☞ In 1990, it split into the Green Party of England and Wales, the Scottish Green Party and the Green Party in Northern Ireland.

☞ The core belief of all three parties is the need to protect the environment, but they added a strong anti-poverty stance more recently.

☞ The Green Party of England and Wales elected Caroline Lucas as their first party leader in 2008; she then became an MP in 2010.

☞ Membership of about 55,500 (March 2017).

UK INDEPENDENCE PARTY (UKIP)

☞ Formed in 1993, calling for Britain to leave the European Union.

☞ Under the leadership of Nigel Farage, UKIP won more seats than either Labour or the Conservatives in the European Parliament elections in 2014, securing 27 per cent of the popular vote and a total of 24 MEPs (Members of the European Parliament).

☞ UKIP also secured its first two MPs at Westminster in 2014, when Douglas Carswell and Mark Reckless won by-elections as UKIP candidates after defecting from the Conservative Party.

☞ As a direct result of UKIP's popularity, Conservative prime minister David Cameron committed to an in-out referendum on EU membership, which was held in June 2016. The UK electorate voted to leave the EU by 51.9 to 48.1 per cent.

☞ Membership of around 34,000 (December 2016).

THE OFFICIAL MONSTER RAVING LOONY PARTY

Politics doesn't have to be entirely serious, and thanks to the Official Monster Raving Loony Party in Britain, it often isn't. Founded by the late David (Screaming Lord) Sutch, the party has provided a political home for the eccentric and extrovert since 1983. You will often spot its garishly dressed candidates during TV coverage of elections.

The Loonies rarely gain more than a few hundred votes and normally lose their deposits. They present their policies with their tongues firmly wedged in their cheeks. Silly as they might be, though, they have a ridiculously sensible guide to being a candidate on their website www.loonyparty.com, which sets out almost all you need to know if you ever think of running for elected office, seriously or not. According to 2016 accounts, the party had 153 paid-up members.

NORMALLY WHEN I'M ON HOLIDAY AND I'M ASKED WHAT I DO, I SAY I'M A TRAFFIC WARDEN. THAT MAKES ME MUCH MORE POPULAR.

STEPHEN POUND MP

MAKING A
DIFFERENCE

We've looked at the main political parties and some of their major leaders of the past. We've also seen some of the significant changes in society that have been brought about by politicians. But politics is more than just a spectator sport. It is at its best when more people get involved. Now that you know your way around the British political system, perhaps it's time to play your part in the democratic process? Here, in the pages that follow, are ten ways that you can dip your toe into the political waters and start changing the world.

JOIN A POLITICAL PARTY

The first step is very easy, because with a few clicks you can become part of the democratic process. Joining a party doesn't commit you to doing anything, but it will certainly open up lots of opportunities. You will get to vote in internal party elections, thereby helping to choose candidates and party leaders. It will cost you a few pounds, but you will be helping your party to win.

2

JOIN A NEW MOVEMENT
OR CAMPAIGNING GROUP

Don't like political parties but still want to change things? You are not alone. A growing number of people are getting involved with organisations such as 38 Degrees and Citizens UK to lobby politicians about issues that concern them. Campaigning organisations like Amnesty International, Greenpeace and Friends of the Earth will always welcome new members, supporters and volunteers. Find out who's campaigning on the issues you care most about and join in.

3

BE PERSISTENT

Local political parties and campaigning groups are mostly run by well-meaning volunteers in their spare time. They are sometimes slightly disorganised and might not immediately come rushing round to your door once your membership subscription has been received. If you want to get involved, you will need to be proactive and not give up just because you think the first person you speak to is a few macaroons short of a coffee morning. Offer to organise a stall in the high street or a fundraising event and they'll be eternally grateful.

4

DELIVER LEAFLETS

Most political parties will have a few leaflets that need delivering, especially around election time, and volunteering to help will make you immediately popular with your party's organisers. It might feel a bit mundane, but it is great exercise and a wonderful way to nosy around your neighbourhood.

5

GO OUT CANVASSING

Knocking on doors is the bread and butter of political activists. It makes a real difference to people's voting behaviour too. A group of academics conducted an experiment in which they found two identical tower blocks in Dundee and canvassed one, but only delivered leaflets to the other. The block where they had knocked on doors had a 10 per cent higher voter turnout as a result. Different parties will canvass in different ways, but it is a lot easier than it looks and can be fun too.

6

CLICKTAVISM

Social media is becoming more and more important in the political world, and there are increasing numbers of political activists creating easily shareable material. Blogging or vlogging can be a great way to engage in the political debate. If you want to avoid irritating your friends and relations too much, though, you might want to set up separate social media accounts just for your political activities.

7

GO TO A PARTY CONFERENCE

The political parties each gather once a year, often in seaside towns beginning with 'B', like Brighton, Bournemouth and Blackpool. You can listen to great speeches and some not so good ones, debate policies and plan campaigns. There will be fringe meetings and training sessions where you can delve further into policy and tactics. They can be expensive to attend and different parties have different rules about who can attend and vote, but it is worth doing at least once in your life. If you are very ambitious and hobnob with the right people, a barnstorming speech from the conference podium could launch a glittering political career.

8

STAND FOR THE COUNCIL

Most political parties are desperate for new people to put themselves forward for election to their local councils. If you care about your local services and can string a few words together into a half-decent speech, you may just find yourself on the ballot paper and perhaps even getting elected. Being a local councillor is a wonderful way of participating in politics, as it gives you a chance to speak up for your local community and really get things done.

9

GO ON A DEMO

It is said that 80 per cent of success in life is about showing up, and it couldn't be truer than in politics. Turning up for a demonstration is a great way to make your point, show your support and catch the attention of others who might join you on your campaign. Designing your own banner with some brightly coloured paint and a witty slogan might even get you into the national press.

10

TRY SOMETHING COMPLETELY NEW

Finally, the best thing about politics is that if you don't like the way things are being done now, you can change it. Finding new ways to campaign and organise, forming new parties or transforming old ones is what keeps politics alive and interesting. So, if you want to try something new, go ahead and have a go. You never know, you might just be on to something.

Acknowledgements

It is customary, at the end of any election count, for the candidates to thank the returning officers and the police for the smooth running of the election and then to thank their agents and campaign teams. The more magnanimous and well mannered will also thank their opponents for a robust but good-natured contest.

So I would like to take this opportunity to thank everyone whom I have campaigned with or against over the years. To the leaflet-deliverers, the canvassers, the candidates, the agents, the party leaders, the spin-doctors and everyone in between – you have all helped to make politics for me a huge pleasure. I would also like to thank all the lovely people at Summersdale for giving me the opportunity to share some of my passion for politics in this little book.

About the Author

Steven Gauge got into politics early in life, leading a small demo around his nursery-school playground. A local councillor at 23 and a parliamentary candidate by 30, he has been a winning election agent and toured the country by battle-bus with party leaders. Author of *Political Wit* (also published by Summersdale), he now works in Westminster, advising businesses, charities and others on how to engage with their elected representatives and navigate through choppy political waters.

Image Credits

The ——

LITTLE BOOK OF

GOING GREEN

Harriet Dyer

THE LITTLE BOOK OF
GOING GREEN

Harriet Dyer

£6.99
Paperback
ISBN: 978-1-78685-491-9

The Little Book of Going Green aims to shed light on the ways humans are harming the environment, from pollution and deforestation to industrial production and farming methods. Filled with facts, theories and tips on how we can do our bit for the planet, this is your one-stop guide to making every aspect of your life earth-friendly.

The
LITTLE BOOK OF
FEMINISM

Harriet Dyer

THE LITTLE BOOK OF
FEMINISM

Harriet Dyer

£5.99

Paperback

ISBN: 978-1-84953-844-2

Do you want to know more about the fight for women's rights, what we've achieved and how we got there? This helpful little guide will teach you the history, theory, big issues and everything you need to know to become a card-carrying feminist.

— The —
LITTLE BOOK OF
VEGANISM

Elanor Clarke

THE LITTLE BOOK OF
VEGANISM

Elanor Clarke

£5.99

Paperback

ISBN: 978-1-84953-759-9

There are plenty of reasons to embrace veganism – for environmental, ethical or health reasons, and many more! This easy-to-digest guide, packed with practical tips on vegan living, from food and drink to clothes and shopping, will inspire you to enjoy all that's best about an ethical and animal-free lifestyle.

POLITICAL

Wit

QUIPS AND QUOTES
FROM THE BACK
BENCHES AND BEYOND

STEVEN GAUGE

POLITICAL WIT

Steven Gauge

£9.99

Hardback

ISBN: 978-1-84953-676-9

Order, order! After a long day at the dispatch box, when your honourable friend's white paper has made you feel green and your poll ratings have slumped to a new low, hunker down in Speakers' Corner with this grand coalition of political quips and quotes – you'll be ready to take on Jeremy Paxman again in no time!

If you're interested in finding out more
about our books, find us on Facebook at
SUMMERSDALE PUBLISHERS and follow us on
Twitter at **@SUMMERSDALE**.

WWW.SUMMERSDALE.COM